Richly textured pattern stitches create decorator pillows with great style. These eight designs feature light, medium, and bulky weight yarns for Easy to Intermediate skill levels.

Contents

LEISURE ARTS, INC.
Maumelle, Arkansas

Tempting *Texture*

Finished Size: 20" (51 cm) square

●●○○ **EASY**

Shopping List

Yarn (Medium Weight) MEDIUM 4

[3.5 ounces, 205 yards (100 grams, 187 meters) per skein]:

☐ Main Color (Blue) - 4 skeins

[1.75 ounces, 115 yards (50 grams, 105 meters) per skein]:

☐ Contrasting Color (Silver) - 3 skeins

Crochet Hook

☐ Size H (5 mm) **or** size needed for gauge

Additional Supplies

☐ Pillow form - 20" (51 cm) square

GAUGE INFORMATION

In Back pattern,
14 dc and 7 rows = 4" (10 cm)
Gauge Swatch: 4" (10 cm) square
With Main Color, ch 16.
Row 1: Dc in fourth ch from hook **(3 skipped chs count as first dc)** and in each ch across: 14 dc.
Rows 2-7: Ch 3 **(counts as first dc)**, turn; dc in next dc and in each dc across.
Finish off.

STITCH GUIDE

SINGLE CROCHET 3 TOGETHER
(abbreviated sc3tog)
Pull up a loop in each of next 3 dc, YO and draw through all 4 loops on hook **(counts as one sc)**.

FRONT

With Contrasting Color, ch 69.

Row 1 (Right side)**:** Sc in second ch from hook and in each ch across: 68 sc.

Note: Loop a short piece of yarn around any stitch to mark Row 1 as **right** side and bottom edge.

Row 2: Ch 1, turn; sc in each sc across changing to Main Color in last sc made ***(Fig. 1a, page 45)***; cut Contrasting Color.

Row 3: Ch 3 **(counts as first dc, now and throughout)**, turn; 2 dc in same st, 3 dc in next sc and in each sc across: 204 dc.

Rows 4 and 5: Ch 3, turn; dc in next dc and in each dc across.

Row 6: Ch 1, turn; beginning in first dc, sc3tog across changing to Contrasting Color in last sc made; do **not** cut Main Color, carry loosely along edge: 68 sc.

Row 7: Ch 1, turn; sc in each sc across.

Row 8: Ch 1, turn; sc in each sc across changing to Main Color in last sc made; cut Contrasting Color.

Rows 9-62: Repeat Rows 3-8, 9 times; at end of Row 62, do **not** change colors.

Finish off.

BACK

With Main Color, ch 70.

Row 1 (Right side)**:** Dc in fourth ch from hook **(3 skipped chs count as first dc)** and in each ch across: 68 dc.

Note: Mark Row 1 as **right** side and bottom edge.

Rows 2-35: Ch 3, turn; dc in next dc and in each dc across.

Finish off.

JOINING

Hold **wrong** sides and bottom edges of Front and Back together. With Front facing and working through **both** layers, join Contrasting Color with sc in first top corner ***(see Joining With Sc, page 45)***; sc in each st across, † ch 1; work 68 sc evenly spaced across end of rows, (ch 1, turn; sc in each sc across) twice, ch 1, slip st in end of next row †; working in free loops of beginning ch ***(Fig. 3b, page 46)***, sc in each ch across, insert pillow form, repeat from † to † once; join with slip st to first sc, finish off.

Design by Mary Beth Temple.

Loop-De-Loop

Finished Size: 16" (40.5 cm) diameter

EASY +

Shopping List

Yarn (Light Weight) LIGHT 3

[3.5 ounces, 245 yards (100 grams, 224 meters) per skein**]**:

- ☐ Color A (Blue) - 5 skeins
- ☐ Color B (Green) - 1 skein
- ☐ Color C (Ecru) - 1 skein

Crochet Hook

- ☐ Size F (3.75 mm) **or** size needed for gauge

Additional Supplies

- ☐ Pillow form - 16" (40.5 cm) diameter
- ☐ Split ring markers - 6

GAUGE INFORMATION

Gauge Swatch: 2½" (6.25 cm) diameter

Work same as Back through Rnd 5: 30 sc.

BACK

With Color A, ch 3; join with slip st to form a ring.

Rnd 1 (Right side)**:** Ch 1, 6 sc in ring; do **not** join, place marker to indicate beginning of rnd ***(see Markers, page 45)***.

Note: Loop a short piece of yarn around any stitch to mark Rnd 1 as **right** side.

Rnd 2: 2 Sc in each sc around: 12 sc.

Rnd 3: (2 Sc in next sc, sc in next sc) around: 18 sc.

Rnd 4: ★ 2 Sc in next sc, place split ring marker around first sc of 2-sc group just made, sc in next 2 sc; repeat from ★ around: 24 sc.

Rnds 5-34: ★ 2 Sc in marked sc, remove marker and place around first sc of 2-sc group just made, sc in each sc across to next marker; repeat from ★ around: 204 sc.

Rnd 35: Sc in each sc around; slip st in next sc; finish off.

FRONT

With Color A, ch 3; join with slip st to form a ring.

Rnd 1 (Right side)**:** Ch 1, 6 sc in ring; join with slip st to first sc.

Note: Mark Rnd 1 as **right** side.

Rnd 2: Ch 1, 2 sc in each sc around; join with slip st to first sc: 12 sc.

Rnd 3: Ch 1, 2 sc in same st as joining, sc in next sc, (2 sc in next sc, sc in next sc) around; join with slip st to first sc: 18 sc.

Rnd 4: Ch 1, 2 sc in same st as joining, sc in next 2 sc, (2 sc in next sc, sc in next 2 sc) around; join with slip st to Front Loop Only of first sc ***(Fig. 2, page 46)***: 24 sc.

Rnd 5 (Begin ruffle)**:** Ch 3 **(counts as first dc, now and throughout)**, **turn**; working in Back Loops Only, 2 dc in same st, 3 dc in next sc and in each sc around; join with slip st to first dc: 72 dc.

Rnd 6: Ch 3, do **not** turn; working in both loops, dc in same st and in next dc, (2 dc in next dc, dc in next dc) around; join with slip st to first dc, finish off: 108 dc.

Rnd 7 (Finish ruffle)**:** With **right** side facing, join Color C with slip st in any dc; ch 2, slip st in second ch from hook, ★ slip st in next 2 dc, ch 2, slip st in second ch from hook; repeat from ★ around to last dc, slip st in last dc; join with slip st to joining slip st, finish off.

When working the Front, it is recommended to join the yarn in different areas to keep the Front circular.

Rnd 8: With **right** side facing and working **behind** Ruffle in free loops on Rnd 4 ***(Fig. 3a, page 46)***, join Color A with sc in any sc ***(see Joining With Sc, page 45)***; sc in same st, place split ring marker around first sc of 2-sc group just made, sc in next 3 sc, ★ 2 sc in next sc, place split ring marker around first sc of 2-sc group just made, sc in next 3 sc; repeat from ★ around; join with slip st to first sc: 30 sc.

Rnds 9-11: Ch 1, ★ 2 sc in marked sc, remove marker and place around first sc of 2-sc group just made, sc in each sc across to next marker; repeat from ★ around; join with slip st to first sc: 48 sc.

Rnd 12: Ch 1, ★ 2 sc in marked sc, remove marker and place around first sc of 2-sc group just made, sc in each sc across to next marker; repeat from ★ around; join with slip st to Front Loop Only of first sc: 54 sc.

Rnd 13 (Begin ruffle)**:** Ch 3, **turn**; working in Back Loops Only and removing markers, 2 dc in same st, 3 dc in next sc and in each sc around; join with slip st to first dc: 162 dc.

Rnd 14: Ch 3, do **not** turn; working in both loops, dc in same st and in next dc, (2 dc in next dc, dc in next dc) around; join with slip st to first dc, finish off: 243 dc.

Rnd 15 (Finish ruffle)**:** With **right** side facing, join Color B with slip st in any dc; ch 2, slip st in second ch from hook, ★ slip st in next 2 dc, ch 2, slip st in second ch from hook; repeat from ★ around; join with slip st to joining slip st, finish off.

Rnd 16: With **right** side facing and working **behind** Ruffle in free loops on Rnd 12, join Color A with sc in any sc; sc in same st, place split ring marker around first sc of 2-sc group just made, sc in next 8 sc, ★ 2 sc in next sc, place split ring marker around first sc of 2-sc group just made, sc in next 8 sc; repeat from ★ around; join with slip st to first sc: 60 sc.

Rnds 17-22: Repeat Rnds 9-14; at end of Rnd 22, do **not** finish off: 378 dc.

Rnd 23 (Finish ruffle)**:** Ch 2, **turn**; slip st in second ch from hook, ★ slip st in next 2 dc, ch 2, slip st in second ch from hook; repeat from ★ around to last dc, slip st in last dc; join with slip st to joining slip st, finish off.

Rnd 24: With **right** side facing and working **behind** Ruffle in free loops on Rnd 20, join Color A with sc in any sc; sc in same st, place split ring marker around first sc of 2-sc group just made, sc in next 13 sc, ★ 2 sc in next sc, place split ring marker around first sc of 2-sc group just made, sc in next 13 sc; repeat from ★ around; join with slip st to first sc: 90 sc.

Rnds 25-30: Repeat Rnds 9-14: 513 dc.

Rnd 31: With Ecru, repeat Rnd 15.

Rnd 32: With **right** side facing and working **behind** Ruffle in free loops on Rnd 28, join Color A with sc in any sc; sc in same st, place split ring marker around first sc of 2-sc group just made, sc in next 18 sc, ★ 2 sc in next sc, place split ring marker around first sc of 2-sc group just made, sc in next 18 sc; repeat from ★ around; join with slip st to first sc: 120 sc.

Rnds 33-38: Repeat Rnds 9-14: 648 dc.

Rnd 39: With Color B, repeat Rnd 7.

Rnd 40: With **right** side facing and working **behind** Ruffle in free loops on Rnd 36, join Color A with sc in any sc; sc in same st, place split ring marker around first sc of 2-sc group just made, sc in next 23 sc, ★ 2 sc in next sc, place split ring marker around first sc of 2-sc group just made, sc in next 23 sc; repeat from ★ around; join with slip st to first sc: 150 sc.

Rnds 41-46: Repeat Rnds 9-14; at end of Rnd 46, do **not** finish off: 783 dc.

Rnd 47: Repeat Rnd 23.

Rnd 48: With **right** side facing and working **behind** Ruffle in free loops on Rnd 44, join Color A with sc in any sc; sc in same st, place split ring marker around first sc of 2-sc group just made, sc in next 28 sc, ★ 2 sc in next sc, place split ring marker around first sc of 2-sc group just made, sc in next 28 sc; repeat from ★ around; join with slip st to first sc: 180 sc.

Rnds 49-52: Repeat Rnds 9-11 once, then repeat Rnd 9 once **more**: 204 sc.

Rnd 53: Ch 1, sc in same st as joining and in each sc around, removing markers; join with slip st to first sc, do **not** finish off.

JOINING

Ch 1; with **wrong** sides of Front and Back together, Front facing, and working through **both** loops on **both** layers; sc in same st as joining and in each sc around inserting pillow form before closing; join with slip st to first sc, finish off.

Design by Mary Beth Temple.

Snowflake

Finished Size: 13½" (34.5 cm) square

EASY +

Shopping List

Yarn (Medium Weight) 4

[7 ounces, 364 yards (198 grams, 333 meters) per skein]:

☐ 1 skein

Crochet Hook

☐ Size G (4 mm) **or** size needed for gauge

Additional Supplies

☐ Pillow form - 14" (35.5 cm) square, knife-edge

GAUGE INFORMATION

14 sc and 16 rows = 4" (10 cm)

Gauge Swatch: 4" (10 cm) square

Ch 15.

Row 1: Sc in second ch from hook and in each ch across: 14 sc.

Rows 2-16: Ch 1, turn; sc in each sc across.

Finish off.

STITCH GUIDE

FRONT POST DOUBLE CROCHET *(abbreviated FPdc)*

YO, working in **front** of previous row, insert hook from **front** to **back** around post of st indicated *(Fig. 4, page 46)*, YO and pull up a loop even with loops on hook (3 loops on hook), (YO and draw through 2 loops on hook) twice. Skip sc behind FPdc.

FRONT POST CLUSTER *(abbreviated FPcl)* (uses 5 sc)

YO, working in **front** of previous row, insert hook from **front** to **back** around post of st indicated *(Fig. 4, page 46)*, YO and pull up a loop even with loops on hook (3 loops on hook), YO and draw through 2 loops on hook, ★ YO, skip **next** sc on same row, insert hook from **front** to **back** around post of **next** sc, YO and pull up a loop, YO and draw through 2 loops on hook; repeat from ★ once **more**, YO and draw through all 4 loops on hook. Skip sc behind FPcl.

FRONT

Ch 48.

Row 1 (Right side)**:** Sc in second ch from hook and in each ch across: 47 sc.

Note: Loop a short piece of yarn around any stitch to mark Row 1 as **right** side.

Row 2 AND ALL WRONG SIDE ROWS: Ch 1, turn; sc in each st across.

Row 3: Ch 1, turn; sc in first 3 sc, work FPcl beginning around second sc 2 rows **below**, ★ sc in next 9 sc, skip next 5 sts 2 rows **below** (from last FPcl worked) and work FPcl beginning around next sc; repeat from ★ across to last 3 sc, sc in last 3 sc.

Row 5: Ch 1, turn; sc in first sc, work FPdc around first FPcl 2 rows **below**, (sc in next sc, work FPdc around same FPcl 2 rows **below**) twice, ★ sc in next 5 sc, work FPdc around next FPcl 2 rows **below**, (sc in next sc, work FPdc around same FPcl 2 rows **below**) twice; repeat from ★ across to last sc, sc in last sc.

Row 7: Ch 1, turn; sc in first 8 sc, work FPcl beginning around seventh st 2 rows **below**, ★ sc in next 9 sc, skip next 5 sts 2 rows **below** (from last FPcl worked) and work FPcl beginning around next sc; repeat from ★ 2 times **more**, sc in last 8 sc.

Row 9: Ch 1, turn; sc in first 6 sc, work FPdc around first FPcl 2 rows **below**, (sc in next sc, work FPdc around same FPcl 2 rows **below**) twice, ★ sc in next 5 sc, work FPdc around next FPcl 2 rows **below**, (sc in next sc, work FPdc around same FPcl 2 rows **below**) twice; repeat from ★ 2 times **more**, sc in last 6 sc.

Rows 10-53: Repeat Rows 2-9, 5 times; then repeat Rows 2-5 once **more**.

Finish off.

BACK

Ch 48.

Row 1 (Right side)**:** Sc in second ch from hook and in each ch across: 47 sc.

Note: Mark Row 1 as **right** side.

Row 2: Ch 1, turn; sc in each sc across.

Repeat Row 2 until Back measures same as Front, ending by working a **right** side row; do **not** finish off.

ASSEMBLY

Rnd 1: Ch 1, turn; with **wrong** sides of both pieces together, Front facing, matching sts on last row and working through **both** thicknesses, (sc evenly across to next corner, 3 sc in corner) 3 times; insert pillow form, sc evenly across to last corner, 3 sc in last corner; join with slip st to first sc.

Rnd 2: Do **not** turn; ★ working from **left** to **right**, insert hook in st to right of hook ***(Fig. A)***, YO and draw through st and through loop on hook ***(Fig. B*****, reverse slip st made)**; repeat from ★ around; join with slip st to first slip st, finish off.

Fig. A

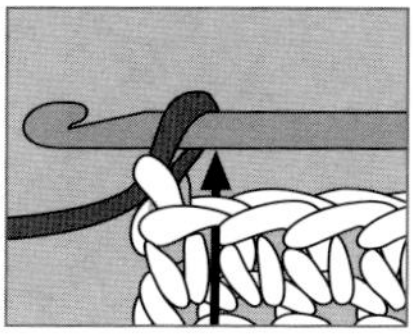

Fig. B

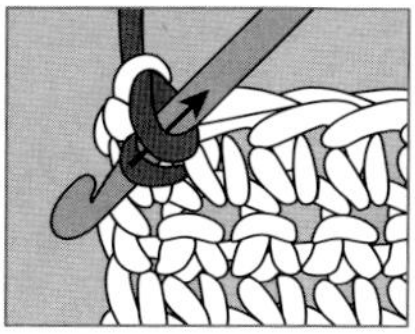

Design by Becky Stevens.

Defined *Waves*

Finished Size: 16" (40.5 cm) square

●●○○ **EASY**

Shopping List

Yarn (Bulky Weight) BULKY 5

[3.5 ounces, 127 yards (100 grams, 116 meters) per skein]:

- ☐ Color A (Gold) - 2 skeins
- ☐ Color B (Purple) - 2 skeins

Crochet Hook

- ☐ Size K (6.5 mm) **or** size needed for gauge

Additional Supplies

- ☐ Pillow form - 16" (40.5 cm) square
- ☐ Yarn needle

GAUGE INFORMATION

In pattern,

1 repeat (10 sts) = 3¼" (8.25 cm)

Gauge Swatch: 16" (40.75 cm) wide flattened

Work same as Pillow for 5 rnds.

STITCH GUIDE

TREBLE CROCHET

(abbreviated tr)

YO twice, insert hook in sc indicated, YO and pull up a loop (4 loops on hook), (YO and draw through 2 loops on hook) 3 times.

PILLOW

With Color A, ch 51.

Rnd 1: Sc in second ch from hook and in each ch across to last ch, 2 sc in last ch; working in free loops of beginning ch ***(Fig. 3b, page 46)***, sc in next 49 chs; inserting hook from **back** to **front**, join with slip st to both loops of first sc, drop Color A: 100 sc.

Always work the first stitch of a round in the last st made.

Rnd 2 (Right side)**:** With Color B, ch 1, turn; working in Back Loops Only ***(Fig. 2, page 46)***, sc in next 2 sc, hdc in next sc, dc in next 5 sc, hdc in next sc, ★ sc in next 3 sc, hdc in next sc, dc in next 5 sc, hdc in next sc; repeat from ★ around to last sc, sc in last sc; join with slip st to **both** loops of first sc.

Note: Loop a short piece of yarn around any stitch to mark Rnd 2 as **right** side.

Rnd 3: Ch 1, turn; sc in Front Loop Only of each st around; inserting hook from **back** to **front**, join with slip st to **both** loops of first sc, drop Color B.

Rnd 4: Turn; with Color A and working in Back Loops Only, slip st in next sc, ch 4 **(counts as first tr)**, tr in next sc, dc in next sc, hdc in next sc, sc in next 3 sc, hdc in next sc, dc in next sc, ★ tr in next 3 sc, dc in next sc, hdc in next sc, sc in next 3 sc, hdc in next sc, dc in next sc; repeat from ★ around to last sc, tr in last sc; join with slip st to first tr.

Rnd 5: Ch 1, turn; sc in Front Loop Only of each st around; inserting hook from **back** to **front**, join with slip st to both loops of first sc, drop Color A.

Rnd 6: With Color B, ch 1, turn; working in Back Loops Only, sc in next 2 sc, hdc in next sc, dc in next sc, tr in next 3 sc, dc in next sc, hdc in next sc, ★ sc in next 3 sc, hdc in next sc, dc in next sc, tr in next 3 sc, dc in next sc, hdc in next sc; repeat from ★ around to last sc, sc in last sc; join with slip st to **both** loops of first sc.

Repeat Rnds 3-6 for pattern until Pillow measures approximately 14½" (37 cm) from beginning ch, ending by working Rnd 5.

Next 2 Rnds: Repeat Rnds 2 and 3.

Last Rnd: Ch 1, turn; sc in Back Loop Only of each st around; join with slip st to **both** loops of first sc, finish off leaving a long end for sewing.

Insert pillow form.

Working through **both** loops of **both** sides, whipstitch top edge together *(**Fig. 7a, page 47**)*.

Design by Darla Sims.

Enclosure

Finished Size: 16" (40.5 cm) square

EASY

Shopping List

Yarn (Bulky Weight) BULKY 5

[3.5 ounces, 127 yards (100 grams, 116 meters) per skein]:

- ☐ Color A (Orchid) - 2 skeins
- ☐ Color B (Grey) - 2 skeins
- ☐ Color C (Ecru) - 2 skeins

Crochet Hook

- ☐ Size K (6.5 mm) **or** size needed for gauge

Additional Supplies

- ☐ Pillow form - 16" (40.5 cm) square

GAUGE INFORMATION

In pattern,
2 repeats = 3½" (9 cm)

Gauge Swatch: 5¼" (13.25 cm) wide flattened

With Color C, ch 18.

Rnds 1-3: Work same as Pillow: 18 ch-1 sps.

Finish off.

STITCH GUIDE

CLUSTER (uses one st or sp)

★ YO, insert hook in st or sp indicated, YO and pull up a loop, YO and draw through 2 loops on hook; repeat from ★ once **more**, YO and draw through all 3 loops on hook.

PILLOW

With Color C, ch 54.

Rnd 1 (Right side)**:** Sc in second ch from hook and in each ch across to last ch, 3 sc in last ch; working in free loops of beginning ch ***(Fig. 3b, page 46)***, sc in next 51 chs, 2 sc in next ch; drop Color C, with Color A, join with slip st to first sc ***(Fig. 1b, page 45)***: 108 sc.

Note: Loop a short piece of yarn around any stitch to mark Rnd 1 as **right** side.

Rnd 2: Ch 1, turn; sc in last sc made, skip next 2 sc, work Cluster in next sc, (ch 1, work Cluster in same st) twice, skip next 2 sc, ★ sc in next sc, skip next 2 sc, work Cluster in next sc, (ch 1, work Cluster in same st) twice, skip next 2 sc; repeat from ★ around; drop Color A, with Color C, join with slip st to first sc: 18 sc and 18 Cluster groups.

Work in the following color sequence:
★ One row **each** Color C, Color B, Color C, Color A; repeat from ★ for color sequence.

Rnd 3: Turn; slip st in sp **before** next Cluster ***(Fig. 5, page 47)***, ch 4 **(counts as first dc plus ch 1)**, working **around** dc just made ***(Fig. 6a, page 47)***, dc in sp **before** joined sc, ch 1, skip next Cluster, sc in next Cluster, ch 1, ★ skip next Cluster and next sc, dc in sp **before** next Cluster, ch 1, working **around** dc just made, dc in sp **before** skipped sc, ch 1, skip next Cluster, sc in next Cluster, ch 1; repeat from ★ around; drop yarn, with next color, join with slip st to first dc: 54 ch-1 sps.

Rnd 4: Ch 1, turn; skip next ch-1 sp ★ sc in next sc, skip next ch-1 sp, work Cluster in next ch-1 sp, (ch 1, work Cluster in same sp) twice, skip next ch-1 sp; repeat from ★ around; drop yarn, with next color, join with slip st to first sc: 18 sc and 18 Cluster groups.

Repeat Rnds 3 and 4 for pattern until Pillow measures approximately 16" (40.5 cm) from beginning ch, ending by working Rnd 3.

Finish off leaving a long end for sewing.

Insert pillow form.

Working through **both** loops of **both** sides, whipstitch top edge together ***(Fig. 7a, page 47)***.

Design by Darla Sims.

Chinese Puzzle

Finished Size: 16" (40.5 cm) diameter

EASY

Shopping List

Yarn (Bulky Weight) BULKY 5

[4 ounces, 124 yards (113 grams, 113 meters) per skein]:

☐ 4 skeins

Crochet Hook

☐ Size K (6.5 mm) **or** size needed for gauge

Additional Supplies

☐ Pillow form - 16" (40.5 cm) square

GAUGE INFORMATION

In pattern, 1 repeat (7 sts) = 2½" (6.25 cm)

Gauge Swatch: 5" (12.75 cm) wide flattened

Ch 14.

Rnds 1-3: Work same as Pillow, page 26: 28 sts (4 dc groups).

Finish off.

STITCH GUIDE

DOUBLE CROCHET 5 TOGETHER
(abbreviated dc5tog)
(uses next 5 sc)
★ YO, insert hook in **next** sc, YO and pull up a loop, YO and draw through 2 loops on hook; repeat from ★ 4 times **more**, YO and draw through all 6 loops on hook **(counts as one st)**.

FRONT POST DOUBLE CROCHET 5 TOGETHER
(abbreviated FPdc5tog)
(worked across next 5-dc group)
★ YO, insert hook from **front** to **back** around post of **next** dc ***(Fig. 4, page 46)***, YO and pull up a loop, YO and draw through 2 loops on hook; repeat from ★ 4 times **more**, YO and draw through all 6 loops on hook **(counts as one st)**.

PILLOW

Ch 42.

Rnd 1 (Right side)**:** 2 Sc in second ch from hook, sc in each ch across to last ch, 3 sc in last ch; working in free loops of beginning ch ***(Fig. 3b, page 46)***, sc in next 40 chs; join with slip st to first sc: 84 sc.

Note: Loop a short piece of yarn around any stitch to mark Rnd 1 as **right** side.

Rnd 2: Ch 3 **(counts as first dc, now and throughout)**, 4 dc in same st, dc5tog, ch 1, skip next sc, ★ 5 dc in next sc, dc5tog, ch 1, skip next sc; repeat from ★ around; join with slip st to first dc: 84 sts (12 dc groups).

Rnd 3: Turn; slip st in last ch made, ch 3, 4 dc in same st, skip next st, work FPdc5tog, ch 1, ★ 5 dc in next ch, skip next st, work FPdc5tog, ch 1; repeat from ★ around; join with slip st to first dc.

Repeat Rnd 3 for pattern until Pillow measures approximately 16" (40.5 cm) from beginning ch.

Finish off leaving a long end for sewing.

Insert pillow form.

Working through **both** loops of **both** sides, whipstitch top edge together ***(Fig. 7a, page 47)***.

Design by Darla Sims.

Mock Cable *Diamond*

Shown on page 28.

Finished Size: 12¼" (31 cm) square

●●○○ EASY +

Shopping List

Yarn (Medium Weight) MEDIUM 4

[7 ounces, 364 yards (198 grams, 333 meters) per skein]:

☐ 1 skein

Crochet Hook

☐ Size G (4 mm) **or** size needed for gauge

Additional Supplies

☐ Pillow form - 14" (35.5 cm) square, knife-edge

GAUGE INFORMATION

14 sc and 16 rows = 4" (10 cm)
Gauge Swatch: 4" (10 cm) square
Ch 15.
Row 1: Sc in second ch from hook and in each ch across: 14 sc.
Rows 2-16: Ch 1, turn; sc in each sc across.
Finish off.

STITCH GUIDE

FRONT POST DOUBLE CROCHET ***(abbreviated FPdc)***
YO, working in **front** of previous row, insert hook from **front** to **back** around post of st indicated ***(Fig. 4, page 46)***, YO and pull up a loop even with loops on hook (3 loops on hook), (YO and draw through 2 loops on hook) twice. Skip st behind FPdc.

FRONT POST CLUSTER ***(abbreviated FPcl)*** (uses one st)
★ YO, working in **front** of previous row, insert hook from **front** to **back** around post of st indicated ***(Fig. 4, page 46)***, YO and pull up a loop even with loops on hook, YO and draw through 2 loops on hook; repeat from ★ once **more**, YO and draw through all 3 loops on hook. Skip st behind FPcl.

POPCORN (uses one sc)
4 Dc in sc indicated, drop loop from hook, insert hook from **front** to **back** in first dc of 4-dc group, hook dropped loop and draw through st.

FRONT

Ch 44.

Row 1 (Right side)**:** Sc in second ch from hook and in each ch across: 43 sc.

Note: Loop a short piece of yarn around any stitch to mark Row 1 as **right** side.

Row 2: Ch 1, turn; sc in each sc across.

Row 3: Ch 1, turn; sc in first 9 sc, † work FPdc around sc one row **below** next sc, (sc in next sc, work FPdc around sc one row **below** next sc) twice †, sc in next 6 sc, work FPcl around sc one row **below** next sc, sc in next sc, work FPcl around sc one row **below** next sc, sc in next 6 sc, repeat from † to † once, sc in last 9 sc.

Row 4 AND ALL WRONG SIDE ROWS: Ch 1, turn; sc in each st across.

Row 5: Ch 1, turn; sc in first 9 sc, † work FPdc around FPdc one row **below** next sc, (sc in next sc, work FPdc around FPdc one row **below** next sc) twice †, sc in next 5 sc, work FPcl around next FPcl 2 rows **below**, sc in next 3 sc, work FPcl around next FPcl 2 rows **below**, sc in next 5 sc, repeat from † to † once, sc in last 9 sc.

Row 7: Ch 1, turn; sc in first 9 sc, † work FPdc around FPdc one row **below** next sc, (sc in next sc, work FPdc around FPdc one row **below** next sc) twice †, sc in next 4 sc, work FPcl around next FPcl 2 rows **below**, sc in next 5 sc, work FPcl around next FPcl 2 rows **below**, sc in next 4 sc, repeat from † to † once, sc in last 9 sc.

Row 9: Ch 1, turn; sc in first 9 sc, † work FPdc around FPdc one row **below** next sc, (sc in next sc, work FPdc around FPdc one row **below** next sc) twice †, sc in next 3 sc, work FPcl around next FPcl 2 rows **below**, sc in next 3 sc, work Popcorn in next sc, sc in next 3 sc, work FPcl around next FPcl 2 rows **below**, sc in next 3 sc, repeat from † to † once, sc in last 9 sc.

Row 11: Ch 1, turn; sc in first 9 sc, † work FPdc around FPdc one row **below** next sc, (sc in next sc, work FPdc around FPdc one row **below** next sc) twice †, sc in next 4 sc, work FPcl around next FPcl 2 rows **below**, sc in next 5 sc, work FPcl around next FPcl 2 rows **below**, sc in next 4 sc, repeat from † to † once, sc in last 9 sc.

Row 13: Ch 1, turn; sc in first 9 sc, † work FPdc around FPdc one row **below** next sc, (sc in next sc, work FPdc around FPdc one row **below** next sc) twice †, sc in next 5 sc, work FPcl around next FPcl 2 rows **below**, sc in next 3 sc, work FPcl around next FPcl 2 rows **below**, sc in next 5 sc, repeat from † to † once, sc in last 9 sc.

Row 15: Ch 1, turn; sc in first 9 sc, † work FPdc around FPdc one row **below** next sc, (sc in next sc, work FPdc around FPdc one row **below** next sc) twice †, sc in next 6 sc, work FPcl around next FPcl 2 rows **below**, sc in next sc, work FPcl around next FPcl 2 rows **below**, sc in next 6 sc, repeat from † to † once, sc in last 9 sc.

Rows 16-51: Repeat Rows 4-15, 3 times.

Finish off.

BACK

Ch 44.

Row 1 (Right side)**:** Sc in second ch from hook and in each ch across: 43 sc.

Note: Mark Row 1 as **right** side.

Row 2: Ch 1, turn; sc in each sc across.

Repeat Row 2 until Back measures same as Front, ending by working a **right** side row; do **not** finish off.

ASSEMBLY

Rnd 1: Ch 1, turn; with **wrong** sides of **both** pieces together, Front facing, matching sts on last row and working through **both** thicknesses, (sc evenly across to next corner, 3 sc in corner) 3 times; insert pillow form, sc evenly across to last corner, 3 sc in last corner; join with slip st to first sc.

Rnd 2: Do **not** turn; ★ working from **left** to **right**, insert hook in st to right of hook (***Fig. A***), YO and draw through st and through loop on hook (***Fig. B*, reverse slip st made**); repeat from ★ around; join with slip st to first slip st, finish off.

Fig. A

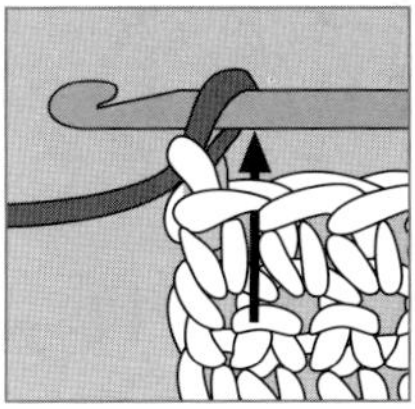

Fig. B

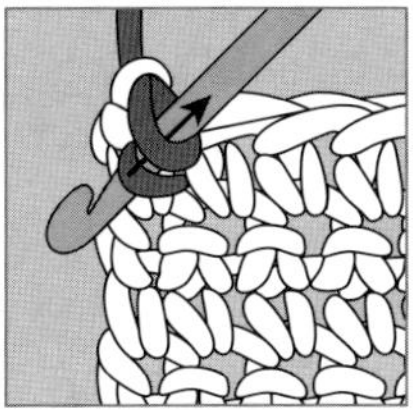

Design by Becky Stevens.

Cabled Bolster

Finished Size: 14" long x 5" diameter (35.5 cm x 12.5 cm)

●●●○ **INTERMEDIATE**

Shopping List

Yarn (Medium Weight) MEDIUM 4

[3.5 ounces, 170 yards (100 grams, 156 meters) per skein]:

- ☐ Color A (Blue) - 1 skein
- ☐ Color B (Brown) - 1 skein
- ☐ Color C (Ecru) - 1 skein
- ☐ Color D (Pink) - 1 skein

Crochet Hooks

- ☐ Size G (4 mm)
- ☐ Size H (5 mm) **or** sizes needed for gauge
- ☐ Bolster pillow form - 14" long x 5" diameter (35.5 cm x 12.5 cm) **or** polyester stuffing
- ☐ Yarn needle

GAUGE INFORMATION

With larger size hook,
14 sc and 16 rows = 4" (10 cm)

Gauge Swatch: 4" (10 cm) square
With larger size hook and Color A, ch 15.

Row 1: Sc in second ch from hook and in each ch across: 14 sc.

Rows 2-16: Ch 1, turn; sc in each sc across.

Finish off.

STITCH GUIDE

FRONT POST DOUBLE CROCHET ***(abbreviated FPdc)***

YO, insert hook from **front** to **back** around post of st indicated ***(Fig. 4, page 46)***, YO and pull up a loop (3 loops on hook), (YO and draw through 2 loops on hook) twice. Skip sc behind FPdc.

CLUSTER

★ YO, insert hook from **front** to **back** around post of **next** FPdc in row **below** ***(Fig. 4, page 46)***, YO and pull up a loop, YO and draw through 2 loops on hook; repeat from ★ once **more**, YO and draw through all 3 loops on hook. Skip st behind Cluster.

POPCORN (uses one sc)

5 Sc in next sc, drop loop from hook, insert hook from **front** to **back** in first sc of 5-sc group, hook dropped loop and draw through st. Ch 1 to close.

STRIP #1

With larger size hook and Color A, ch 6.

Row 1 (Right side)**:** Sc in second ch from hook and in each ch across: 5 sc.

Note: Loop a short piece of yarn around any stitch to mark Row 1 as **right** side and bottom edge.

Row 2 AND ALL WRONG SIDE ROWS: Ch 1, turn; sc in each st across.

Row 3: Ch 1, turn; sc in first sc, skip next sc, work FPdc around sc one row **below** next sc, sc in next sc, work FPdc around same st as first FPdc, sc in last sc.

Row 5: Ch 1, turn; sc in first 2 sc, work Cluster, sc in last 2 sc.

Row 7: Ch 1, turn; sc in first sc, skip next sc, work FPdc around top of Cluster in row **below**, sc in next sc, work FPdc around same st as first FPdc, sc in last sc.

Rows 8-74: Repeat Rows 4-7, 16 times; then repeat Rows 4-6 once **more**.

Finish off.

First Side Trim: With **right** side facing, smaller size hook, and working in end of rows, join Color A with sc in last row ***(see Joining With Sc, page 45)***; work 71 sc evenly spaced across; finish off: 72 sc.

Second Side Trim: With **right** side facing, smaller size hook, and working in end of rows, join Color A with sc in first row; work 71 sc evenly spaced across; finish off: 72 sc.

STRIP #2

With larger size hook and Color B, ch 13.

Row 1: Sc in second ch from hook and in each ch across: 12 sc.

Note: Mark **back** of any st on Row 1 as **right** side and bottom edge.

Rows 2-5: Ch 1, turn; sc in each sc across.

Row 6 (Right side)**:** Ch 1, turn; sc in first 5 sc, skip next sc, work FPdc around sc one row **below** next sc, working in **front** of FPdc just made ***(Fig. 6b, page 47)***, work FPdc around sc one row **below** skipped sc, sc in last 5 sc.

Row 7 AND ALL WRONG SIDE ROWS: Ch 1, turn; sc in each st across.

When working FPdc around FPdc, work in row **below** previous row.

Row 8: Ch 1, turn; sc in first 4 sc, work FPdc around next FPdc, sc in next 2 sc, work FPdc around next FPdc, sc in last 4 sc.

Row 10: Ch 1, turn; sc in first 3 sc, work FPdc around next FPdc, sc in next 4 sc, work FPdc around next FPdc, sc in last 3 sc.

Row 12: Ch 1, turn; sc in first 2 sc, work FPdc around next FPdc, sc in next 2 sc, skip next sc, work FPdc around sc one row **below** next sc, working in **front** of FPdc just made, work FPdc around sc one row **below** skipped sc, sc in next 2 sc, work FPdc around next FPdc, sc in last 2 sc.

Row 14: Ch 1, turn; sc in first sc, work FPdc around next FPdc, (sc in next 2 sc, work FPdc around next FPdc) across to last sc, sc in last sc.

Row 16: Ch 1, turn; sc in first 2 sc, work FPdc around next 2 FPdc, sc in next 4 sc, work FPdc around next 2 FPdc, sc in last 2 sc.

Row 18: Ch 1, turn; sc in first 2 sc, † skip next FPdc, work FPdc around next FPdc, working in **front** of FPdc just made, work FPdc around skipped FPdc †, sc in next 4 sc, repeat from † to † once, sc in last 2 sc.

Row 20: Ch 1, turn; sc in each sc across.

Rows 22-66: Repeat Rows 6-21 twice; then repeat Rows 6-18 once **more**.

Rows 67-70: Ch 1, turn; sc in each sc across; at end of Row 70, do **not** finish off.

Change to smaller size hook.

First Side Trim: Ch 1, do **not** turn; working in end of rows, work 72 sc evenly spaced across; finish off.

Second Side Trim: With **right** side facing, smaller size hook, and working in end of rows, join Color B with sc in first row; work 71 sc evenly spaced across; finish off: 72 sc.

STRIP #3

With larger size hook and Color C, ch 10.

Row 1 (Right side)**:** Sc in second ch from hook and in each ch across: 9 sc.

Note: Mark Row 1 as **right** side and bottom edge.

Rows 2-4: Ch 1, turn; sc in each sc across.

Row 5: Ch 1, turn; sc in first 3 sc, work Popcorn, work FPdc around sc one row **below** next 2 sc, sc in last 3 sc.

Row 6 AND ALL WRONG SIDE ROWS: Ch 1, turn; sc in each st across.

When working FPdc around FPdc, work in row **below** previous row.

Row 7: Ch 1, turn; sc in first 3 sc, work FPdc around next 2 FPdc, sc in last 4 sc.

Row 9: Ch 1, turn; sc in first 2 sc, work FPdc around next 2 FPdc, sc in last 5 sc.

Row 11: Ch 1, turn; sc in first sc, work FPdc around next 2 FPdc, sc in last 6 sc.

Row 13: Ch 1, turn; sc in first sc, work FPdc around next 2 FPdc, work Popcorn, sc in last 5 sc.

Row 15: Ch 1, turn; sc in first 2 sc, work FPdc around next 2 FPdc, sc in last 5 sc.

Row 17: Ch 1, turn; sc in first 3 sc, work FPdc around next 2 FPdc, sc in last 4 sc.

Row 19: Ch 1, turn; sc in first 4 sc, work FPdc around next 2 FPdc, sc in last 3 sc.

Row 21: Ch 1, turn; sc in first 3 sc, work Popcorn, work FPdc around next 2 FPdc, sc in last 3 sc.

Rows 22-69: Repeat Rows 6-21, 3 times.

Rows 70-72: Ch 1, turn; sc in each sc across.

Finish off.

First Side Trim: With **right** side facing, smaller size hook, and working in end of rows, join Color C with sc in last row; work 71 sc evenly spaced across; finish off: 72 sc.

Second Side Trim: With **right** side facing, smaller size hook, and working in end of rows, join Color C with sc in first row; work 71 sc evenly spaced across; finish off: 72 sc.

STRIP #4

With larger size hook and Color D, ch 16.

Row 1: Sc in second ch from hook and in each ch across: 15 sc.

Row 2 (Right side)**:** Ch 1, turn; sc in first 5 sc, work Popcorn, sc in next 3 sc, work Popcorn, sc in last 5 sc.

Note: Mark Row 2 as **right** side and bottom edge.

Row 3 AND ALL WRONG SIDE ROWS: Ch 1, turn; sc in each st across.

Row 4: Ch 1, turn; sc in first 4 sc, work FPdc around top of next Popcorn, work FPdc around next sc one row **below**, sc in next sc, work Popcorn, sc in next sc, work FPdc around sc one row **below** last sc worked into, work FPdc around top of next Popcorn, sc in last 4 sc.

When working FPdc around FPdc, work in row **below** previous row.

Row 6: Ch 1, turn; sc in first 3 sc, work FPdc around next 2 FPdc, sc in next 5 sc, work FPdc around next 2 FPdc, sc in last 3 sc.

Row 8: Ch 1, turn; sc in first 2 sc, work FPdc around next 2 FPdc, sc in next 7 sc, work FPdc around next 2 FPdc, sc in last 2 sc.

Row 10: Ch 1, turn; sc in first 3 sc, work FPdc around next 2 FPdc, sc in next 5 sc, work FPdc around next 2 FPdc, sc in last 3 sc.

Row 12: Ch 1, turn; sc in first 4 sc, work FPdc around next 2 FPdc, sc in next sc, work Popcorn, sc in next sc, work FPdc around next 2 FPdc, sc in last 4 sc.

Row 14: Ch 1, turn; sc in first 5 sc, work Popcorn, sc in next 3 sc, work Popcorn, sc in last 5 sc.

Rows 15-73: Repeat Rows 3-14, 4 times; then repeat Rows 3-13 once **more**.

Finish off.

First Side Trim: With **right** side facing, smaller size hook, and working in end of rows, join Color D with sc in last row; work 71 sc evenly spaced across; finish off: 72 sc.

Second Side Trim: With **right** side facing, smaller size hook, and working in end of rows, join Color D with sc in first row; work 71 sc evenly spaced across; finish off: 72 sc.

STRIP #5

With larger size hook and Color A, ch 9.

Row 1 (Right side)**:** Sc in second ch from hook and in each ch across: 8 sc.

Note: Mark Row 1 as **right** side and bottom edge.

Row 2: Ch 1, turn; sc in each st across.

Row 3: Ch 1, turn; sc in first 2 sc, work FPdc around sc one row **below** next 4 sc, sc in last 2 sc.

Row 4: Ch 1, turn; sc in each st across.

When working FPdc around FPdc, work in row **below** previous row.

Row 5: Ch 1, turn; sc in first 2 sc, skip next 2 FPdc, work FPdc around next 2 FPdc, working in **front** of FPdc just made, work FPdc around each skipped FPdc, sc in last 2 sc.

Rows 6 and 7: Repeat Rows 4 and 5.

Row 8: Ch 1, turn; sc in each st across.

Row 9: Ch 1, turn; sc in first 2 sc, work FPdc around next 4 FPdc, sc in last 2 sc.

Rows 10-15: Repeat Rows 8 and 9, 3 times.

Rows 16-73: Repeat Rows 4-15, 4 times; then repeat Rows 4-13 once **more**; do **not** finish off.

Change to smaller size hook.

First Side Trim: Ch 1, do **not** turn; work 72 sc evenly spaced across end of rows; finish off.

Second Side Trim: With **right** side facing, smaller size hook, and working in end of rows, join Color A with sc in first row; work 71 sc evenly spaced across; finish off: 72 sc.

FIRST END

Rnd 1 (Right side)**:** With larger size hook and Color D, ch 2, 8 sc in second ch from hook; do **not** join, place marker to indicate beginning of rnd ***(see Markers, page 45)***.

Rnd 2: 2 Sc in each sc around: 16 sc.

Rnd 3: (2 Sc in next sc, sc in next sc) around: 24 sc.

Rnd 4: (2 Sc in next sc, sc in next 2 sc) around: 32 sc.

Rnd 5: (2 Sc in next sc, sc in next 3 sc) around: 40 sc.

Rnd 6: (2 Sc in next sc, sc in next 4 sc) around: 48 sc.

Rnd 7: Sc in each sc around.

Rnd 8: (2 Sc in next sc, sc in next 5 sc) around; slip st in next sc, finish off: 56 sc.

Rnd 9: With **right** side facing, join Color C with sc in same st as slip st; sc in each sc around; place marker.

Rnd 10: (Sc in next sc, work Popcorn) around.

Rnd 11: Sc in next 2 sts, 2 sc in next st, sc in next 3 sts, ★ 2 sc in next st, (sc in next 2 sts, 2 sc in next st) twice, sc in next 3 sts; repeat from ★ around; slip st in next sc, finish off leaving a long end for sewing: 72 sc.

POPCORN

With larger size hook and Color C, ch 2, work Popcorn in second ch from hook; finish off leaving a long end for sewing.

Sew Popcorn to **right** side at center of Rnd 1.

SECOND END

Work same as First End using Color B for Rnds 1-8.

ASSEMBLY

Join Strips in numerical order using photo, page 38, as a guide for placement.

With **right** sides facing, having bottom edges at same end and using smaller size hook, join Strips as follows:

Working in **inside** loops of sc on Trim on **both** Strips ***(Fig. A)***, join Color C with slip st in first sc; holding yarn to back of work, slip st in next sc and in each sc across; finish off.

Fig. A

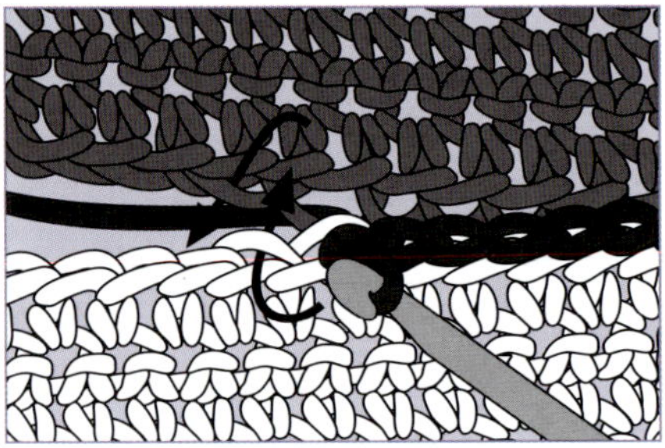

Fold piece in half matching last rows to beginning chs. Using corresponding color yarn and working in inside loops, whipstitch across to form a tube ***(Fig. 7b, page 47)***.

Trim: With **right** side facing, join Color C with sc in first sc on Trim on either outer Strip; sc in each sc around; join with slip st to first sc, finish off.

Repeat Trim on opposite side.

With Color C, whipstitch First End to tube (closest to Strip #1).

Insert pillow form **or** stuff with polyester fiberfill.

Whipstitch Second End in same manner.

Design by Darla Sims.

General *Instructions*

ABBREVIATIONS

ch	chain(s)
cm	centimeters
dc	double crochet(s)
dc5tog	double crochet 5 together
FPcl	Front Post cluster
FPdc	Front Post double crochet(s)
FPdc5tog	Front Post double crochet(s) 5 together
hdc	half double crochet(s)
mm	millimeters
Rnd(s)	Round(s)
sc	single crochet(s)
sc3tog	single crochet 3 together
sp(s)	space(s)
st(s)	stitch(es)
tr	treble crochet(s)
YO	yarn over

SYMBOLS & TERMS

★ — work instructions following ★ as many **more** times as indicated in addition to the first time.

† to † — work all instructions from first † to second † **as many** times as specified.

( ) or **[ ]** — work enclosed instructions **as many** times as specified by the number immediately following **or** work all enclosed instructions in the stitch or space indicated **or** contains explanatory remarks.

colon (:) — the number(s) given after a colon at the end of a row or round denote(s) the number of stitches or spaces you should have on that row or round.

CROCHET TERMINOLOGY		
UNITED STATES		INTERNATIONAL
slip stitch (slip st)	=	single crochet (sc)
single crochet (sc)	=	double crochet (dc)
half double crochet (hdc)	=	half treble crochet (htr)
double crochet (dc)	=	treble crochet (tr)
treble crochet (tr)	=	double treble crochet (dtr)
double treble crochet (dtr)	=	triple treble crochet (ttr)
triple treble crochet (tr tr)	=	quadruple treble crochet (qtr)
skip	=	miss

CROCHET HOOKS																	
U.S.	B-1	C-2	D-3	E-4	F-5	G-6	7	H-8	I-9	J-10	K-10½	L-11	M/N-13	N/P-15	P/Q	Q	S
Metric - mm	2.25	2.75	3.25	3.5	3.75	4	4.5	5	5.5	6	6.5	8	9	10	15	16	19

●○○○ **BEGINNER**	Projects for first-time crocheters using basic stitches. Minimal shaping.
●●○○ **EASY**	Projects using yarn with basic stitches, repetitive stitch patterns, simple color changes, and simple shaping and finishing.
●●●○ **INTERMEDIATE**	Projects using a variety of techniques, such as basic lace patterns or color patterns, mid-level shaping and finishing.
●●●● **EXPERIENCED**	Projects with intricate stitch patterns, techniques and dimension, such as non-repeating patterns, multi-color techniques, fine threads, small hooks, detailed shaping and refined finishing.

Yarn Weight Symbol & Names	LACE 0	SUPER FINE 1	FINE 2	LIGHT 3	MEDIUM 4	BULKY 5	SUPER BULKY 6	JUMBO 7
Type of Yarns in Category	Fingering, size 10 crochet thread	Sock, Fingering, Baby	Sport, Baby	DK, Light Worsted	Worsted, Afghan, Aran	Chunky, Craft, Rug	Super Bulky, Roving	Jumbo, Roving
Crochet Gauge* Ranges in Single Crochet to 4" (10 cm)	32-42 sts**	21-32 sts	16-20 sts	12-17 sts	11-14 sts	8-11 sts	6-9 sts	5 sts and fewer
Advised Hook Size Range	Steel*** 6 to 8, Regular hook B-1	B-1 to E-4	E-4 to 7	7 to I-9	I-9 to K-10½	K-10½ to M/N-13	M/N-13 to Q	Q and larger

*GUIDELINES ONLY: The chart above reflects the most commonly used gauges and hook sizes for specific yarn categories.

** Lace weight yarns are usually crocheted with larger hooks to create lacy openwork patterns. Accordingly, a gauge range is difficult to determine. Always follow the gauge stated in your pattern.

*** Steel crochet hooks are sized differently from regular hooks–the higher the number, the smaller the hook, which is the reverse of regular hook sizing.

GAUGE

Exact gauge is **essential** for proper size. Before beginning your pillow, make the sample swatch given in the individual instructions in the yarn and hook specified. After completing the swatch, measure it, counting your stitches and rows or rounds carefully. If your swatch is larger or smaller than specified, **make another, changing hook size to get the correct gauge**. Keep trying until you find the size hook that will give you the specified gauge.

MARKERS

Markers are used to help distinguish the beginning of each round being worked. Place a 2" (5 cm) scrap piece of yarn before the first stitch of each round, moving marker after each round is complete.

JOINING WITH SC

When instructed to join with sc, begin with a slip knot on hook. Insert hook in stitch or space indicated, YO and pull up a loop, YO and draw through both loops on hook.

CHANGING COLORS

To change colors while working a sc, pull up a loop in stitch indicated (2 loops on hook), drop yarn, hook new yarn ***(Fig. 1a)*** and draw through both loops on hook.

Fig. 1a

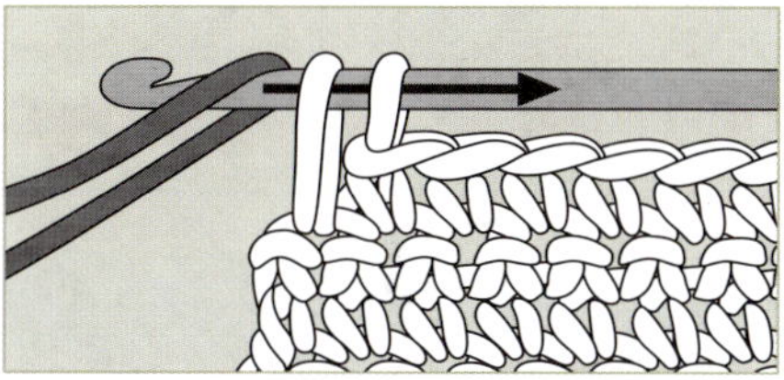

To change colors while joining with a slip st, drop yarn, insert hook in first stitch, hook new yarn and draw through st and loop on hook ***(Fig. 1b)***.

Fig. 1b

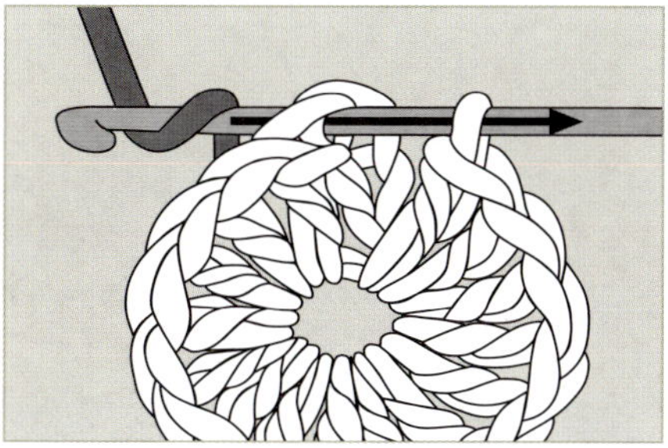

BACK & FRONT LOOP ONLY

Work only in loop(s) indicated by arrow ***(Fig. 2)***.

Fig. 2

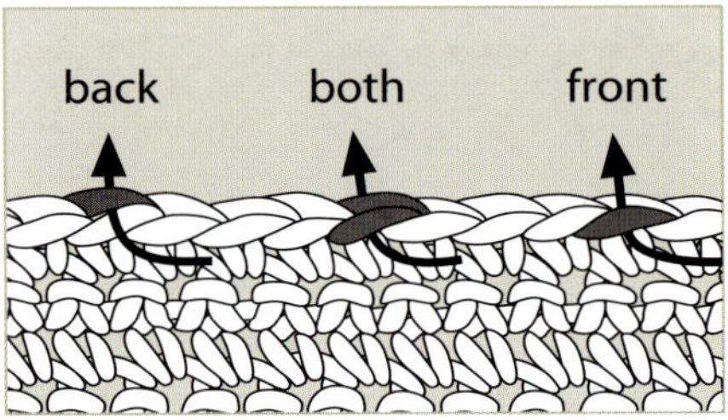

FREE LOOPS

After working in Back or Front Loops Only on a row or round, there will be a ridge of unused loops called the free loops. Later, when instructed to work in the free loops of the same row or round, work in these loops ***(Fig. 3a)***.

Fig. 3a

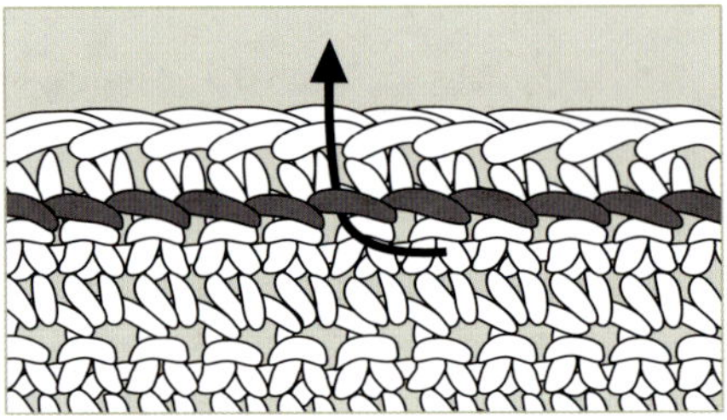

When instructed to work in free loops of a chain, work in loop indicated by arrow ***(Fig. 3b)***.

Fig. 3b

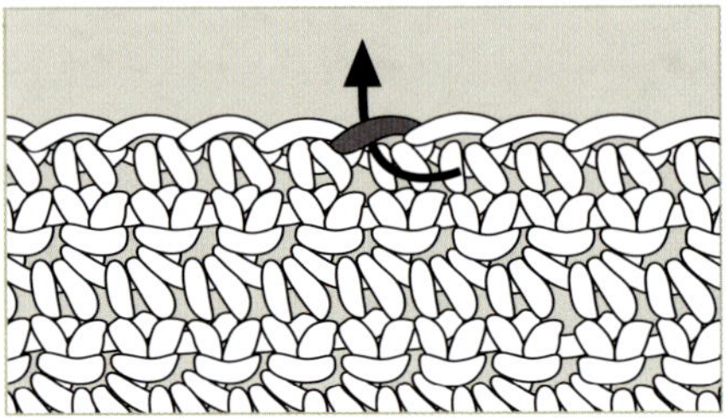

POST STITCH

Work around post of stitch indicated, inserting hook in direction of arrow ***(Fig. 4)***.

Fig. 4

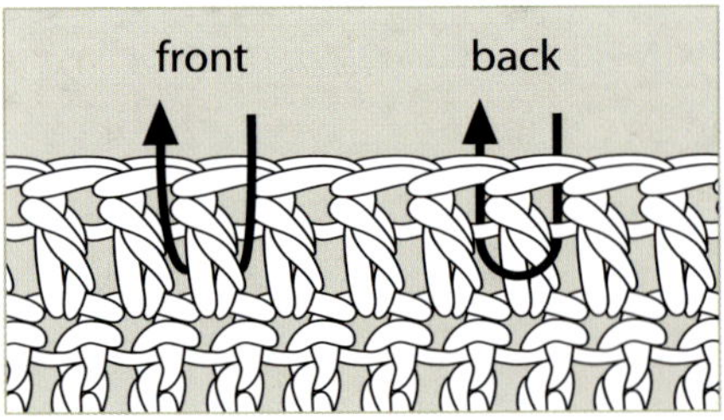

WORKING IN SPACE BEFORE A STITCH

When instructed to work in space before a stitch or in spaces between stitches, insert hook in space indicated by arrow ***(Fig. 5)***.

Fig. 5

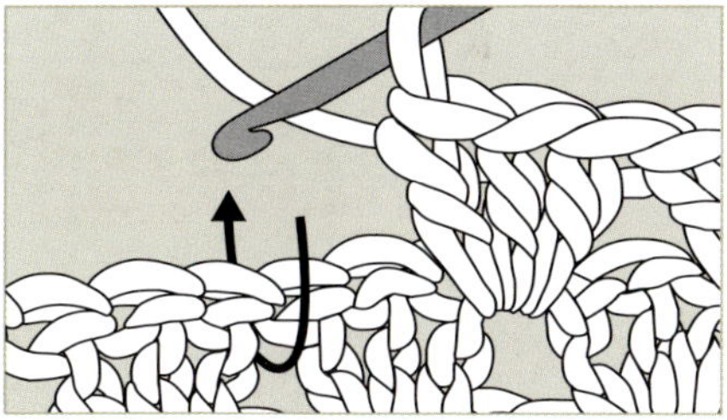

WORKING AROUND OR IN FRONT OF A STITCH

Work in stitch indicated, inserting hook in direction of arrow ***(Figs. 6a & b)***.

Fig. 6a

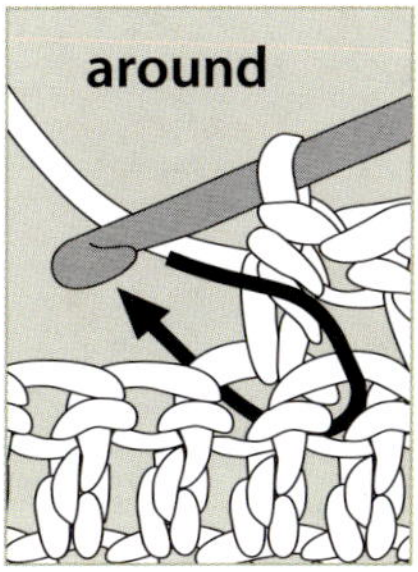

Fig. 6b

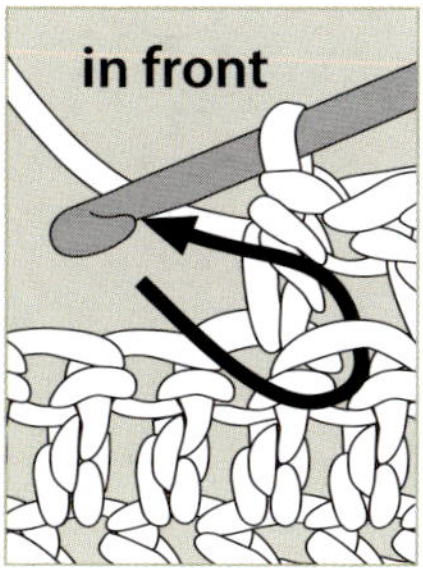

WHIPSTITCH

With **wrong** sides together, sew through both pieces once to secure the beginning of the seam, leaving an ample yarn end to weave in later. Insert the needle from **right** to **left** through **both** loops on **both** pieces ***(Fig. 7a)*** **or** through **inside** loops only of each stitch on **both** pieces ***(Fig. 7b)***. Bring the needle around and insert it from **right** to **left** through the next strand on both pieces. Repeat along the edge, being careful to match stitches and rows.

Fig. 7a

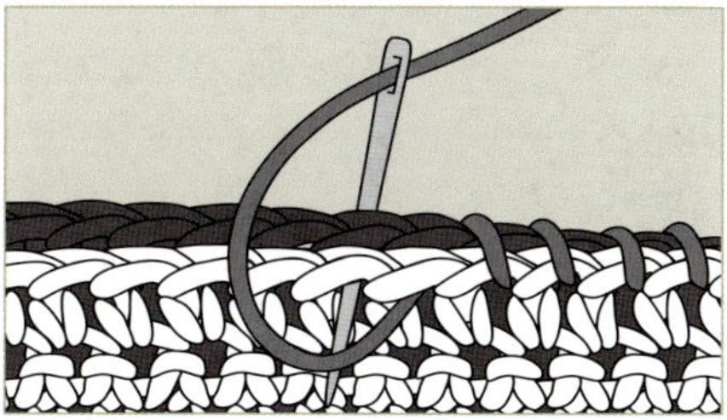

Fig. 7b

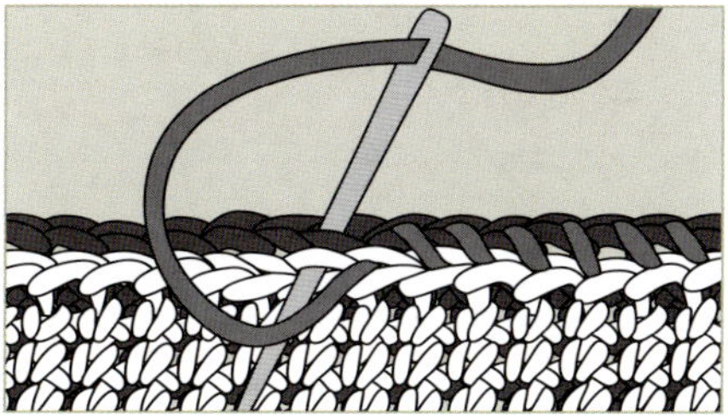

YARN INFORMATION

The pillows in this book were made using a variety of yarns. Any brand of the specific weight of yarn may be used. It is best to refer to the yardage/meters when determining how many balls or skeins to purchase. Remember, to arrive at the finished size, it is the GAUGE/TENSION that is important, not the brand of yarn.

For your convenience, listed below are the yarns used to create our photography models. Because yarn manufacturers make frequent changes in their product lines, you may sometimes find it necessary to use a substitute yarn or to search for the discontinued product at alternate suppliers (locally or online).

TEMPTING TEXTURE
Patons® Canadiana™
Main Color - #10134 Royal Blue
Lion Brand® Glitterspun®
Contrasting Color - #150 Silver

LOOP-DE-LOOP
Lion Brand Collection® Cotton Bamboo
Color A - #107 Hyacinth
Color B - #174 Snapdragon
Color C - #098 Magnolia

SNOWFLAKE
Red Heart® Super Saver®
#313 Aran

DEFINED WAVES
Lion's Pride® Woolspun®
Color A - #130 Honey
Color B - #147 Purple

ENCLOSURE
Lion's Pride® Woolspun®
Color A - #142 Orchid
Color B - #150 Oxford Grey
Color C - #098 Fisherman

CHINESE PUZZLE
Lion Brand® Wool-Ease® Tonal
#187 Buttercup

MOCK CABLE DIAMOND
Red Heart® Super Saver®
#313 Aran

CABLED BOLSTER
Lion Brand® Vanna's Choice®
Color A- #109 Colonial Blue
Color B - #125 Taupe
Color C - #098 Fisherman
Color D - #101 Pink

We have made every effort to ensure that these instructions are accurate and complete. We cannot, however, be responsible for human error, typographical mistakes, or variations in individual work.

Instructions tested and photo models made by Raymelle Greening.

Production Team: Writer/Technical Editor - Cathy Hardy; Editorial Writer - Susan Frantz Wiles; Senior Graphic Artist - Lora Puls; Graphic Artist - Leia Morshedi; Photo Stylist - Stephanie Moore; and Photographer - Jason Masters.